You Deserve Life

❧

Karen Wright-Chisolm,
A.A., B.S., M.S.

Karen Wright-Chisolm
#1 Best Selling Author

Lynn Wright - Thanks

#1 Best Selling Author

ABOUT THE COVER!

The author acknowledges the blurriness of the photograph is used to emulate or realize the uncertainties of life. We live each day, not knowing our fate from the time we are awaken in the mornings or even if we will open our eyes to see another day. We are not promised another day, not even another second or minute. It is only God's Grace that gives us the faith to believe that it is the decision of the Almighty God if we receive another chance or get to see another day. Yet, it is because of our FAITH in GOD that I wanted to write this book entitled: "You Deserve Life!"

Posted February 17, 2016: "TooCuteForCancer is feeling grateful with LaToya Wright" posted Feb. 17, 2016. LaToya passed approximately 3 months later on May 9, 2016. These are the words posted by Latoya in one of the last post she published on Facebook. This book is being dedicated to the life and legacy of LaToya Wright. Her battle was with cancer and not domestic violence, however, her FAITH IN GOD proved that even though Cancer took her life –

SHE deserved life as God kept her.

#usemylife "It's time to stop playing y'all! One year ago today I was diagnosed with stage 4 cancer. There comes a time in your life when you have to really come out of the things that bind you. It's not like you don't have the power, you just don't enforce it. We pray over and over, God do this, God do that, but He is telling you, "child it's already done". When you finally come to a place when the arm of God is revealed to you, you better act like you know! He is in you and you have HIS power but you have to remain close to Him to operate in it. It's time to start walking in the authority that He has given you. Speak over your life, your mind, your body, your family and PLEASE by all means BELIEVE that which you speak. Any doubt that you allow to creep in and make comfortable will destroy your chances. The tongue is powerful so be careful what you speak into the atmosphere. The things and people that don't speak life/positivity should be avoided. God allowed me to be diagnosed with cancer because he had a plan for MY life. I had no choice but to sacrifice my life for the things that I claimed I wanted, there was no way around it. It comes with a price. You all have no idea what He is doing for me in my life right now! Cancer got my attention but I'm about to put that chick to bed! I am currently walking into my destiny. Now I'm about to Milly Rock and two step it all the way out. I'm in good hands. Stay tuned! #usemylife #stillhere #toocute4cancer*"

Rest In Peace My Angel – We All Love And Miss You

ACKNOWLEDGEMENT

Whereas you do not know what will happen tomorrow.
For what is your life? It is even a vapor that appears for
a little time and then vanishes away. James 4:14

O death, where is thy sting? O grave, where is thy victory? The sting of death is sin; and the strength of sin is the law. But thanks be to God, which giveth us the victory through our Lord Jesus Christ (1 Corinthians 15:55-57 KJV). We, who have lived and gained wisdom of the power of God, can now understand the fact that we are all born into this world and one day we will all die. It is my hope that the life I live will leave remnants in the hearts of those who knew me. It is my prayer that my life, my stories, my experiences and my testimonies will help someone struggling through life to understand and realize that God gives us life and an opportunity to experience life to the full extent. Because God sacrificed His life for each of us, it is my confirmation to know that, I too Deserve Life, regardless of what plans Satan may have for our lives, be it, sickness of the body, sickness of the mind or even sickness of the heart, "**You Deserve Life**". I have experienced death of so many that came in different forms; however, I know and understand that it does not matter what experiences we face; the word of God gives us the courage to walk into, walk through it and to be victorious in the eyes of God. The secrets of my life that held me bondage for over 27 years finally gave me the inspiration to share in an effort to help myself, as well as others to heal. It is a true saying that, "You Don't Know My Story". But, because I know and I trust the word of God, I am committed to tell everyone about the love of God and ALL He has done for me. "Therefore, my dear brothers and sisters, stand firm. Let nothing move you. Always give yourselves fully to the work of the Lord, because you know that your labor in the Lord is not in vain" (1 Corinthians 15:58 KJV).

You Deserve Life!!

"Never Underestimate The Power of Someone Else's Struggles Unless You Have Walked In Their Shoes" Karen Wright-Chisolm

KAREN WRIGHT-CHISOLM,
A.A., B.S., M.S.

Scriptures marked NIV are taken from the New International Version*. Copyright @ 1973, 1978, 1984, 2011 by Biblica, Inc.". All rights reserved. Scriptures marked NKJV are taken from the New King James Version*. Copyright @ 1982 by Thomas Nelson All rights reserved. Printed in the United States of America ISBN:

ISBN: 978-1-7377290-7-5

For more information on the content of this book, email: kjwrightchisolm@gmail.com
JMPinckney Publishing Company, LLC
104 Berkeley Square Lane
PMB 28
Goose Creek, South Carolina 29445

Cover Design: Michael D. Hall
First printing October 2021 / Printed in the United States of America

DEDICATION

This book is being dedicated to the life and legacy of Sharon Carter Burnell, my friend. A sweet soul, one who always shared a smile and a word of encouragement, truly a woman that deserved life to the fullest capacity of a good and perfect life lived. A life gone to soon, her memories and legacy of the spirit that she possessed will always remain in my heart. **"You Deserve Life"**

Dedicated to the life of my niece, Tonya Euland Carson who was killed October 3, 2014 by a drunk driver who was fleeing after a domestic violence altercation with his wife. Both he and Tonya were killed instantly. A life taken too soon at the hands of another, we "Trust God" and hold to God's Promises that if we live right we will see her again - **"You Deserve Life"**.

Dedicated to the life and legacy of Nacari, a jewel and a pearl. Loved by all she met. May your life be an inspiration for the young and the old with the assurance that God's love is never ending, "Gone Too Soon"; **"You Deserve Life"** and it is my prayer that you are rejoicing in the heavens with the one who comforts you and keeps you in His bosom forever.

Dedicated to the life and legacy of Lillie Mae Dawson Canty Hill. A life well lived, gone too soon. I remember the talks, the laughs and the tears we shared with one another. Whenever we would talk we found comfort in each other's misery, sorrows and love. Take your Rest, you will always be in my heart and in my memories. Love you forever.... **"You Deserve Life"**

Dedicated to the life and legacy of Chessington Marshall, killed by her boyfriend in a domestic violence dispute. **"You Deserve Life"** Dedicated to my nephew, Theron Bernard Hamilton killed in a domestic violence situation by his estranged girlfriend in New York City. Gone too soon. **"You Deserve Life"** Dedicated to the life of my niece, LaToya who fought Stage 4 Cancer with the Love of God in her daily life and who gracefully walked into Heaven without a "Fear". God Bless her soul. **"You Deserve Life"** Dedicated to life and legacy of Myra Singleton Thompson killed at the hands of a killer with no regard for human life, killed 9 people in the Emanuel 9 shooting. Myra was a sweet soul with so much love and compassion for family and friends. R.I.P. Myra, we love you; but God loves you best. **"You Deserve Life"** In Loving Memory Of Caleb Amir "Mook" Brown March 20, 2000 ~ Dec. 5, 2012 "PURPOSE DRIVEN" Because we understand and believe that God does not make any mistakes, our hearts are reminded that God in His infinite wisdom knew that you had completed your purpose here on earth and decided on December 5, 2012 it was time for you to come home. We did not understand why God would take you after only 12 years on earth. But, as I mediated on Numbers 14:24 which reads "But because my servant Caleb has a different spirit and follows me wholeheartedly, I will bring him into the land he went to, and his descendants will inherit it". I began to understand that the number twelve represents completion, you are "God's Servant" and He knew you were ready and even though we love you and miss you God Loves You Best, Rest in Peace my Angel, we will see you in the morning. "You Deserve Life"

"Truly, truly, I say to you, an hour is coming, and is now here, when the dead will hear the voice of the Son of God, and those who hear will live. For as the Father has life in Himself, so He has granted the Son also to have life in Himself. And he has given Him authority to execute judg-

ment, because He is the Son of Man. Do not marvel at this, for an hour is coming when all who are in the tombs will hear His voice and come out, those who have done good to the resurrection of life, and those who have done evil to the resurrection of judgment. John 5:25-29

FOREWORD

I met Karen Wright-Chisolm over 5 years ago. She was my supervisor: we became friends and now we are Sisters in Christ. During this time, we have laughed, cried, been there for each other in the worst of times and the best of times. When I loss my husband, she was there from his diagnose until he passed. After he passed, we became traveling buddies, or should I say, she let me tag along. It was during this time when she shared her story with me.

I began to realize what an amazing woman she had become. You see, she has lived through so many situations that the average person would have not made it through, but God! Some of them she cried through, some of them she was guided through, but all of them she prayed through. This book is her life at work. When you read this book, you will see her experiences working in your life. You will gain strength, wisdom, power, but most of all, you will gain knowledge that you can and will make it with the help of God.

Karen Wright-Chisolm has a servant heart. She is willing to help anyone she comes in touch with. She is a leader, mentor, and a friend. Out of these qualities was born "A Centralized Moment - The Focus is YOU." This non-profit organization was birthed out of her vision that every woman "Deserves Life".

This book exemplifies the characteristics of a women who displays leadership, mentorship and spiritual guidance to let women know that despite the struggles we experience daily in our lives, God has declared that HE promises that "**You Deserve Life**"!

Rev. Dr. Cassandra Tutt-Williams

TABLE OF CONTENTS

INTRODUCTION

"Never underestimate the power of someone else's struggles unless you have walked in their shoes. KWC

For such a time as this, we need to focus our minds and hearts on Romans 8. Romans Chapter 8 is one of the most **powerful** and **prophetic** chapters in the Bible. In studying this chapter, it helped me to understand the sufferings that I endured during those years I experienced domestic violence. I thank Almighty God for the experiences of my life and the strength that my testimonies have given to me. God's grace and mercy revealed the embodiment of His love as cascaded images reflecting over my life with the manifestations of how far God has brought me; despite the obstacles and barriers that I experienced in my life. I am truly a better woman, a better Christian and a better Child of God today because of the trials and tribulations that God allowed me to go through. I rejoice today, because I know that if God was not there with me through all the trials, all the bad days, all the good days, all the ups and all the downs, I would not have been able to share my stories with the strength and wisdom that I have today. To God Be The Glory!

"*Encouragement*" according to the word as Paul wrote, that we who know the word of God and God knows and I paraphrase: "*Hold on, for I reckon that the suffering of the present age is not worthy to be compared to the glory which shall be revealed in us*". It is because of

1

God, I am alive today to tell my story to reveal and give God all the Glory, the Honor and ALL the Praise. And because God has spared me, it has been my duty over the past five years to no longer be ashamed to share my story, to not live in silence anymore, to not be ashamed, but to shout and proclaim every opportunity God affords me to tell the world what God has done for me and how God has brought me through; not only the suffering of Domestic Violence, but every suffering that I went through or will go through, I have to share and encourage. For the word says, "let the redeemed of the Lord say so". Always remember, you are a "Child of God". No matter who you are, where you were born, or what circumstances of life you have to deal with daily. God made each of us, and for that reason alone – **"You Deserve Life".**

CHAPTER 1

For I know the plans I have for you," declares the LORD,
"plans to prosper you and not to harm you, plans to
give you hope and a future. Jeremiah 29:11 KJV

"Trust God"

Take 73 seconds – close your eyes. Doesn't seem like a long time when you close your eyes, but that is how often another American is sexually assaulted in the world today.

"You Deserve Life" – suffering is just a season, suffering is just a moment of time, there are moments in our lives that we need to hear from someone that has been there, that have suffered in silence, someone that knows that God will make a way out of no way and that God will bring us through whatever we are going through, and that God can do all, because God has brought me through those seasons in my life when I thought I could not go on; those times when I could not see my way out of my situation, but God brought me through. Because "You Don't Know My Story", you would not understand what I went through, you would not understand how many times I felt that I could not go on, you would not understand how many times I just wanted to give up, you would not know how many times I felt that I would be better off dead rather than go through the things I was going through. You would not understand why I just wanted to end my life, "But God, But God, But God". You don't know how close I was to ending my life, you don't know what I went through, but thank God that His Glory was revealed in me. God gave me a Praise that only I can understand, so when you see me praising God, you may not understand the tears falling from my eyes, because you don't know my story. When my suffering is revealed to the eyes of others, God has fixed it that all you see is God's Glory, all you see are my successes. "For A Time Such As This", when all that is going on around us, we don't believe that we are going to make it. People are losing their jobs and their homes, but we must trust God, because this is just a season… when people are losing their jobs and their homes, just trust God because this is just a season. Remember – suffering and "*weeping may endure for a night, but Joy comes in the morning*". Thanking God that as we share our experiences of what God has brought us through, by sharing our experiences of how God kept us, by sharing our experiences of how God brought us through it would encourage someone else to seek God for faith, for security, and for break-through. In this, we know that we all will suffer in this life, but as long as we trust and understand God, He will bring us through. **"You Deserve Life"** - God has brought you to a time in your life that you must share your sufferings and your experiences with God to strengthen and encourage others. "Know that For Such A Time As This" – God is still in control – God will bring us through. No matter what you see, you must declare that since you know God and believe, **"You Deserve Life"**. You have to suffer before you can see the Glory of God being revealed. Since weeping only endures for a night – keep going – **"You Deserve Life"**. Because you are *More Than A Conqueror*, I know that **"You Deserve Life"**. And I know that after we experience all the evils, all the struggles, all the pain, all the seasons of our life, God will always reveal His Glory!

Growing up in in my neighborhood, we would see situations where families, including my own, experience an argument and sometimes a fight with their spouses; thus; we prepared ourselves for the Friday night action that was bound to happen. The fathers in the neighborhood were all hard workers and took care of their families, so Friday night was the aftermath of celebrating that it was Friday and there was no workday until Monday. I remember times when we would seek refuge at each other's home. We never imagined there was anything wrong with the altercations; we simply thought it was normal for husbands and wives to behave in that manner and stay together. Several of the couples never separated until death did them part. I would often ask the question with my siblings, why do you think Mrs. X let Mr. Y abuse her? We lived through those days and we never spoke about it at school or among our friends. We were always told, what happens in this house stays in this house. We never made fun of one another, because we all experienced it some form or another. Some may have been physically abused, while some were verbally abused.

I reminiscence on the words of the song, "You Don't Know My Story" - The song says if you knew everything that I went through, when you see me and I'm smiling and I'm happy, despite the hurt and the abuse, you would understand why. You would understand that I know who holds my hand, I know who holds my future, I know that the battle is not mine, but it is indeed the LORD's.

Some of you know me, but you really don't know the woman behind the mask that carried her story for over 30 years. God promised me that if I believed in Him and trusted in Him, He would bring me through. The song says, "You Don't Know My Story, because if you did you would just lift up your hands". Deliverance is my testimony.

CHAPTER 2

*1 The LORD is my light and my salvation— whom
shall I fear? The LORD is the stronghold of my life—
of whom shall I be afraid? (Psalm 27:1)*

The Struggle

I was seventeen years old, four months pregnant, and two months away from graduating high school. I was scared to death that my parents, my teachers, and my friends would find out, and that I would not be allowed to graduate. I managed to conceal the truth until five months later, when I delivered my daughter on September 26, 1973. Little did I know that my life would change drastically from that day moving forward. The man who I believed was "the one I would spend the rest of my life with", became a living nightmare. We had been dating and living together for a while when the physical abuse started. Shortly before our daughter was born, he joined the Navy. We were separated for a while, but once he returned, we married. We were married for approximately one year when my son was born. I was excited, believing that a son would settle him down and force him to want to be a model father. I was wrong. His behavior did not change; if anything, it got worse. He began to take my son with him and expose him to acts of drugs and dealing with other women. There was always an argument whenever I inquired of his whereabouts or what he was doing.

For four years, I endured daily verbal and sometimes physical abuse. I never knew what to expect when he would come home from work. He was either high on drugs or intoxicated. I wanted to believe that he wanted to do better, but you guessed it – that never happened. There were times that I would get calls from the police department to come and pick up my children because their father had been taken to jail for shoplifting to support his habit or even for breaking and entering others' homes.

I worked shift-work, so he was usually at home with the children all night. Sometimes, I would get off work in the morning after working shift work to find my children in the custody of my brothers who were called because he had committed a crime and was being taken to jail. I believe that was the situation that broke my heart; the time I got home from work and found out that he was arrested and my children were with my brothers. As I began to search, call and inquire with the police station as to the charges he was facing and why he was arrested, I broke down as I heard the charges being brought against him. Again, I thought he would change, but as I stated before, things just kept getting worse.

I remember so many times before that, he would abuse me, then he would apologize by telling me he was sorry and I would return home. Because of the many outbreaks of arguments and physical abuse, I found myself moving multiple times within that four and a half years, that I lost account of my moves. I remember the rage of jealously anytime there was another man in the presence of our home. The accusations would stimulate an argument even if the males were family members; his brothers or other relatives. I clearly remember times when we had stayed around family members and he began to remove all of my clothes and shoes from the house, in a rage. He spitefully threw them in a dumpster in the front of the community grocery store. I cried for days and could not understand why he got so angry over accusations that were so

7

far from being the truth. As I think about it now, I believe that he kept trying to move further and further away from family in hopes that there was no one around that I could not run to for safety and to help.

God bless his soul. I also remember when I moved to Goose Creek, South Carolina, my now deceased cousin and his now deceased wife would always open the doors to their home whenever I would come. I didn't matter what hour of the night it was, as it happened so many times, they were always welcoming. Whenever I would escape my home and proceed to their home, or whenever I rang the doorbell in the late hours of the night, whenever I would show up in the early morning hours, they would open the door and without me having to utter a word, let me and my children in to safety and a place to stay. I finally realized that this was not the environment I wanted to raise my daughter or my son in. I was living a nightmare. I was afraid to be in the same house with him. Each time the abuse took place, I kept telling myself that he would change, and things would get better, but it never did; therefore, I struggled for over four and a half years trying to sustain and take care of my two children. There were instances where the police were knocking at my door, the children were crying, but I was afraid to press charges against him or turn him in. It was very tough, but I kept trusting and believing that God would not put anymore on me than I could bear.

It was August 1, 1981, when God woke me up – not only from my restless night's sleep, but as it pertained to my life. This was the day that I would begin to transition from a life of domestic violence to a new beginning for myself and for my two children. I will never forget the words that God spoke to me as I sat up in my bed after my, then husband, left for work. God told me that this was the time for me to escape from the tortures of my marriage - pack up and get out.

I immediately jumped out of bed, made two phone calls, and began to pack up all of my possessions. I knew that I had to be packed and out of the house before he returned from work, because if he knew what I was attempting to do, he would never let me leave there alive. I called my brothers and a few of my friends, and we packed the house in less than seven hours. At approximately 2:45 p.m., we pulled away from the house leaving only my ex-husband's clothes in the bedroom closet, hanging all alone.

I wished I could have been a fly on the wall to see the expression on his face as he inserted the key to open the door, only to find the house was empty, and we were gone. He made several attempts to contact me, but I knew that this was the only way I would be able to leave, and I refused to even entertain seeing him or answering his calls. He continued to attempt to contact me for about two weeks. In the past, I had left and returned over and over again, but I knew this time, if I wanted to survive, I should not go back. After his failed attempts, I think he also realized that I was not giving in and coming back this time. This began my transition from a life of regular verbal and physical abuse to living and providing as a separated parent of two children.

After we divorced, I decided that I needed to do something different with my life. I was afraid to get involved with anyone romantically for fear of having to relive the nightmares of the physical and verbal abuse that I had previously experienced. I was still working the job that required me to do shift work, which resulted in me spending lots of hours away from my children. I realized that this was not the lifestyle that I wanted to live, nor did I want to subject my children to it anymore. It was at this time that I began to get my body physically and mentally prepared to enter the United States Air Force Reserves.

Many nights I prayed and I cried out to God to help me make it through the battles that I was going through. Throughout the daily verbal abuse and sometimes dealing with physical abuse, I never stopped praying to God.

There are many, many examples of struggles in the Bible; however, through faith in God and the belief that "*all things work together for good to them who love God, to them who are the called according to His purpose,"* (Romans 8:28 KJV), we can trust that whatever we go through, it is for our good and for the glory of God. In the midst of my struggles, I continued to move forward because of my Faith in God.

CHAPTER 3

23 Don't have anything to do with foolish and stupid arguments, because you know they produce quarrels. 24 And the Lord's servant must not be quarrelsome but must be kind to everyone, able to teach, not resentful. 2 Timothy 2:23-24 KJV

The Struggle Continues

When I decided to join the military, I had been married and divorced, and a single parent raising two children. I had been holding down a steady job, but I realized I wanted to do more with my life. I never imagined the experiences that I would have later in my life, the places I would travel, and the thousands of people I would meet.

Preparing my mind and body for what was about to become the beginning of the rest of my life was quite a process. It took me seven years to situate my children and get my body in shape. I needed this time to regulate my mind to gain the understanding and belief that I could be someone different; something more; someone better, and that the military would give me what I needed to take care of myself and take care of my two children. I entered the military at age thirty-one, but I knew that I had to do what I had to do. My children were separated from me again; however, I knew that it would only be temporary until I returned from Basic

Training. My sisters were very supportive and took care of my children while I was gone.

It took me several years to trust any man, and I continued to be paranoid about being close to a man. Because of the physical and sexual trauma that I experienced, I began to believe that this was normal. I began to wonder if, in fact I was truly worthy of the respect that I desired. As I worked hard to make a better life for myself and a better life for my children, I found myself battling every day against men who tried to push me over the edge with verbal abuse, condescending emails, and daily questioning of my skills and knowledge. Every day, I had to prove myself worthy of success as an African American woman with credentials. This never-ending battle was exhausting-where and when would it end?

I now realize it may have seemed natural for me to marry a man that reminded me of my abusive father. For years, I experienced my dad coming home intoxicated and fighting my mother until he finally decided to leave. Even after they divorced, for years, I witnessed my mother drinking and engaging in relationships with men who were abusive, both physically and verbally.

The few memories from childhood and the history of my family have had a profound impact on the person I am today. I often ask myself, how is it that I only have bits and pieces of my childhood memories? I now believe that the physical abuse that I witnessed for years as a child, growing up in a house where my father was abusive to my mother, caused me to block out memories of growing up. It was not until I began to write down my experiences that I was able to recall memories that were somehow blocked and placed in the back of my mind, but deep in my heart – suppressed! For years, I was mentally drained from continuing to let memories of the physical and mental abuse slide until I decided that I would not and could not take it any longer, and I had reached the end of my rope. I would have flashbacks of my father's friend cornering me in the house until I was finally able to get away; flashbacks of the countless times I had to hide and lock myself and my children in a closet, until my ex-husband fell asleep, to protect us from abusive rants. I endured flashbacks of my training instructor making verbal sexual advances toward me as a way of intimidating me because of my age when I entered the military.

My decision to join the military was to escape my past of domestic violence and the dangers I felt at the time. Yes, I believed that my troubles were over and that I would finally be respected for the woman that I was. My defenses grew stronger as I attempted to prove myself worthy of more than physical, mental, and sexual abuse. Even though I faced challenges – instances of racial and sexual discrimination – I was able to overcome and make it through. I knew if I could overcome sexual trauma as a child and physical and verbal abuse in my marriage, I could overcome anything. Those experiences made me stronger and more determined to survive - **"You Deserve Life"**.

CHAPTER 4

¹²To the rest I say (I, not the Lord) that if any brother has a wife who is an unbeliever, and she consents to live with him, he should not divorce her. ¹³If any woman has a husband who is an unbeliever, and he consents to live with her, she should not divorce him. ¹⁴For the unbelieving husband is made holy because of his wife, and the unbelieving wife is made holy because of her husband. Otherwise your children would be unclean, but as it is, they are holy. ¹⁵But if the unbelieving partner separates, let it be so. In such cases the brother or sister is not enslaved. God has called you to peace. ¹⁶For how do you know, wife, whether you will save your husband? Or how do you know, husband, whether you will save your wife? 1 Corinthians 7:12-16 ESV

My Story is Not Over

I have endured a lot in my life, and people close to me kept telling me, "You need to write a book." I listened, but I continued to put it off until I was reminded, time and time again, that tomorrow is not promised. You should never put off tomorrow those things that you can and need to do now. I believe if I had not joined the military, I would not be as successful as I am today. The military taught me to overcome the many obstacles I endured and made me a better person. I was able to overcome and defeat the negative experiences of my life, and I was determined not to be a statistic of violence, but a statistic of success and endurance.

I turned my struggles into my success. I believe that God had a plan for my life, and if God had not freed me from my struggles, I would not be alive today to tell my story. People see me and think that I have always had it together, but they don't "know my story". Had it not been for the prayers and support of my family, as well as the wisdom of my grandmother and my mother passed on to me, I would have given up and given in a long time ago. I probably would not be alive today to tell my story. I am in awe how God, in His own way, has renewed my spirit and prepared me for the things I needed to do in order to move forward. The last 30 years have been full of constant reminders of how important life is and that each of our lives has a purpose. Because of all the things I experienced in the most recent years of my life, I believe God's purpose for me will be revealed in the life experiences I share in this book. It is my hope that someone can relate to the trials and tribulations that I have endured and realize that, she too, can overcome whatever obstacle she encounters in life. I hope that she believes that she can be successful in whatever she puts her mind to accomplish.

CHAPTER 5

"Being confident of this very thing, that he which hath begun a good work in you will perform it until the day of Jesus Christ." Phil 1:6 KJV

"God Brought Me Through"

This little skinny, nappy-headed girl from "back da Green," born with deformities of club feet, deprived of a "normal" life with both parents, raised primarily by her mother and grandmother, number "seven out of 11 plus one" has finally found herself. I am proud to say I have made it through 27 years, eight months and 14 days of military service. I have achieved the highest rank that only one percent is able to attain, and I achieved the rank after a minimum of 16 years in the military. I was a fast burner and a committed servant to the troops. I am well loved and respected by all I have met. While a single parent, I was able to complete an Associate Degree in Personnel Administration, a Bachelor of Science Degree in Human Resources Management, and a Dual Master's Degree in Human Resources Management/Development. I am currently pursuing a Doctorate of Management Degree in Organizational Leadership, that have all culminated my career as the first black female Chief Master Sergeant to serve as the 315th Military Personnel Chief in the history of the organization at Charleston Air Force Base, South Carolina.

Before I put pen to paper, I pondered over what part of my story I would tell, I became overwhelmed at the many things I could write about. I have since re-married and am happy in the life that I have created for myself, with God's help. I have another child, along with 7 grandchildren and two great grandchildren. Wondering if I did not decide to take charge of my life, I would not have been able to experience the grace and mercies that God had planned for me. I believe that when you read the back-story of how I got here, you will have a greater appreciation and more respect for my journey. So many of us have incredible stories to tell, yet we believe we cannot be successful because of where we come from, our past mistakes, and who we are as a result. Yes, the military played a major role in the person I am today compared to the person I was before I joined. For that I am forever grateful to God for the opportunity.

I am not really sure where these stories will lead me. I not sure how many other lives will be impacted by my story, but what I know for sure is that God has put the vision in my heart and my soul that I need to tell my story. It is my hope and my prayer that other sisters will be able to relate to my story and realize that they too, can be successful. You see me, but can you see my struggles? "Order my steps for God's designated purpose".

CHAPTER 6

"And we also thank God continually because, when you received the word of God, which you heard from us, you accepted it not as a human word, but as it actually is, the word of God, which is indeed at work in you who believe". 1 Thessalonians 2:13 KJV

Because I Believe

As our lives are transposed from childhood to adulthood, I have always believed that everything happens for a reason, and that everyone who is a part of our lives or comes into our lives, is for a purpose. I have experienced a lot of things, from life to death, as well as death to life. The longer I live the more experiences I endure and go through, and the more I realize and understand that God is truly in control. There are so many memories of my childhood that are a bit vague; however, I find myself reliving them. On the contrary, there are also memories, I really needed to forget.

As a child, I experienced a long lasting plunge in my life when my parents found out that I had clubbed feet and needed to wear braces. I was too young to really understand exactly what was wrong. I believed that I was different because of the fact that I had to wear high top brown shoes with braces. I remembered experiencing many sleepless nights lying in a bed with railings and having to wear those high top brown shoes with the heavy braces attached, even while I slept. I believed that the nightmares I had, involved nightmares that my bed was always moving, were a direct result of the braces on my feet. I would wake up in the middle of the night screaming so loudly that the whole house would be awaken… and they were not always in the best mood. No matter how very hard I tried, I was never really able to fall back to sleep until my mother or my father came into the room to comfort me until I fell asleep. My siblings would always make fun of me and tease me that I was cripple and the poster child for the March of Dimes. I heard these words so long that I began to believe what they were saying was true and that I would never walk like normal people, without the use of those high top brown boots and metal braces that went up to my knees.

Because I Believed that God was in control, I survived that stage of my life. I don't really remember exactly what happened, but as I grew older and after numerous trips to the doctors and the hospitals, I was able to let go of the braces and just wear the high brown boots, which after a while also eventually came off. The teasing continued, but I never lost hope or faith. My grandmother treated me like royalty. Whenever my siblings or friends made fun of me, my grandmother would chastise them and urge them to leave me alone. My grandmother gave me the nickname "Peanut". I am not sure why, but her voice and her words would always comfort me. It was those struggles and times that I reflect on that kept me moving forward. Because I believed in those lessons that were taught by my parents, my grandparents and my Sunday school teacher, it has helped me. Just when it seemed like it was the end of the world, "Because I Believed, God healed my body and not only did I loose the braces, but because I Believed, I was able to come out of the high top boots". Was it a miracle? I believed it was. As a small child I always trusted my instincts, as well as paid attention to even the smallest airy feeling I had about something, about anything.

I was only seven years old when I experienced the death of a close family member. My grandmother, whose voice and words would always comfort me, had gone home to be with the Lord. Even though, I don't believe I understood death and what it meant to die at that time, I vividly remembered the night she died. Her death was the first death I experienced of a close family member. My grandmother was my rock and my soul supporter.

It was November 1963 - I will never forget the screams I heard that rustled through the house. The scream of our neighbor, as I knew her then, Mrs. Hester; Mrs. Hester was a woman of big stature, dark skinned, short hair, loud voice, but a heart of gold. It was the darkest part of the night, as I heard her scream – "Liza, Liza, oh Liza! It was then that the whole house was awaken. I am not sure why we were all there in the house at that time, other than it was probably evident to my mother that the time was near for my grandmother's home going. I vaguely remembered us all gathering in the front room, praising God, crying and coming together as a family, but broken and separated by death of the Matriarch of our family. This was the beginning of a long week ahead of us, as in those days, once the funeral parlor picked up the body, the body was embalmed and prepared for viewing, then the body was returned to the home of the deceased where the body remained and lie instate until the day of the funeral. I remember seeing the casket with my grandmother lying there in a deep sleep, as I thought for the next five days; never closing the casket. We stayed in the house for the entire time while we prepared for the day she would be buried. I am not sure if I was too young to understand or if it is just the portions of that time that I remember. We were too young to be afraid or think or believe whether it was a bad thing or a good thing. I recall that every day and every night, people would come to the house and enter into the living room where the body laid in the casket, in front of the window where everyone that poured into the house could see. My grandmother's living room served as the funeral parlor, as we know today as the funeral chapels. Friends and family came to view the body and to pay their respect to the deceased everyday and every night for approximately five-six days, sitting, eating, reminiscing and supporting the family. We looked forward to each day because we knew that someone would bring something good to eat or drink. My mother and aunt did not have to worry about preparing any food for us the entire week, as well as the day of the funeral.

CHAPTER 7

*"The LORD is on my side; I will not fear. What
can man do to me?" Psalm 118:6*

Experiences I will never forget.

It was the day of the funeral, that year as I stated before was 1963.
Because of my age, the younger children in the family were not
allowed to go to the funeral. My family traveled from downtown
Charleston to Jamestown, South Carolina, my grandmother's home-
town, which was about 45-50 minutes from my grandmother's
house. We were too young to understand about death and we were
not able to attend the funeral. While we waited patiently for my
mom and my sisters to return home after the funeral, we decided to
go to the corner store. I will never forget how my older sister, who
was returning home stopped us as we entered the neighborhood
corner store. We frequented this store every day, but this particular
day, she was yelling and waving to prohibit us from going into Mr.
Abe's store because he was a white man and Martin Luther King,
Jr. had just been assassinated; therefore, we were not to patronize
white owned businesses.

Abe was a Jew that we supported and came to know as a friend of
the family. My sister yelled to us not to enter that white man's store

because President John F. Kennedy had just been shot and killed. We were all shocked and surprised at the news and heeded to her plea not to go into the store. All of a sudden, it seemed strange how the word of President John F. Kennedy's assassination, after experiencing my grandmother dying and being buried on the same day of President John F. Kennedy's death, provoked a different meaning or reaction to death. Although I had not realized and or displayed emotions when my grandmother died, I found myself huddled in a group with my brothers and sisters all crying and distraught about the death of President John F. Kennedy.

Because I believed, as I grew older, I watched my grandfather and my parents as family mentors die, each experience being different. However, the understanding of death did not really move me to the point where I felt a void, because both of my parents were always there.

1963 reminded me of several incidents; the dying of the family matriarch of our family, the one that we all so affectionately called "Momma"; the assassination of President John F. Kennedy; and the Civil Rights Movement a year earlier that brought the Rev. Dr. Martin Luther King, Jr., to visit Charleston, South Carolina.

Preceding the assassination of President Kennedy, it was the first time I had heard about the Rev. Dr. Martin Luther King, Jr., who had visited Charleston, South Charleston in the year of 1962. Dr. King attended the Southern Christian Leadership Conference at the Mother Emanuel AME Church in an effort to encourage and urge members of the congregation and the city to register to vote.

Fast-forwarding after the assassination of President John F. Kennedy, it was 1967, and I was 11 years old. I heard that Martin Luther King, Jr. was coming to Charleston, South Carolina for the second time. The first time he came was 1962 and I was too young to remember. I vaguely remembered Dr. King arriving in Charleston, South Carolina in 1967 during the Civil Rights Movement where he made a speech very similar to the speech he made in 1962 to encourage and urge residents to vote. The assassination of President John F. Kennedy put a damper on the black race to the point where Dr. ML King's visit to Charleston, South Carolina was very critical.

In April 1968, the assassination of Rev. Dr. Martin Luther King, Jr., again shone a gloom picture of despair as death again took a seat in the mind of this 12-year-old little girl who still did not really understand why there was so much cruelty in a world where people were dying, and killing one another while others were protesting discrimination because of the color of their skin.

By 1969, Civil Rights was in full bloom in Charleston, South Carolina, when the Nurse's Strike brought focus to Charleston again with Coretta Scott King and Ralph Abernathy. They both led a march with local leaders and supporters in Charleston along with over 400 African American hospital workers that were mostly females. They stood against the all-white administrations of the Medical University of South Carolina Hospital and the Charleston County Hospital. This strike lasted 100 days during the spring and summer season, in a dispute between a debate with employers and employees over civil rights, unionization of public sector workers and gender roles. I learned later that the catalyst for black hospital workers to organize occurred in February of 1967; nearly five years after Rev. Dr. Martin Luther King, Jr., made his first visit to Charleston, SC in 1962.

I was really still too young to understand what was going on around me, but I understood enough to know that my parents, my friend's parents, my grandparents and older members of my community and the surrounding cities supported and respected the Rev. Dr. Martin Luther King, Jr., President John F. Kennedy and other leaders that were around during those times. All of the older people I knew, as well as my older brothers and sisters all participated in the marches, the protesting and the politics of what was going on during these times.

Karen Wright-Chisolm, A.A., B.S., M.S.

Life as we knew it, was based on what we saw our parents and other adults display in our presence. As a child, I had no idea that I would encounter some of those same issues and conflicts that I saw as a child, as an adult. Because I believed in what I witnessed, it prepared me as I grew into adulthood on how to better handle death as it invaded my life.

Several years after my maternal grandmother and grandfather died, my paternal grandfather, who lived in the same house with us, in a one room apartment, passed away in 1973. I was a senior in high school and just about ready to graduate. Still very young, I remember times that my grandfather would only come out of his room to use the bathroom or inject his voice when my father decided he wanted to get drunk and fight with my mother. I knew my grandfather as granddaddy and never inquired about his wife or where she was until I grew older and learned that she had died when I was only two years old. The memories of my grandfather were minimal. I remember he was a soft-spoken, tall, slender and handsome man who wore glasses. We would go into his room and sit with him; however, I don't remember what we talked about. I have memories of my paternal grandfather, as I grew a little older, being sick and my younger brother and I would have to stay in the room with him and attend to his needs. My younger brother spent more time than I did, but I remember him always staying in the room with granddaddy. I don't really remember clearly, but I believe that during this time, my father had moved out of the house and was living somewhere else with his new family. I don't remember why my father never seemed to tend to his father while he was sick or why he was not still part of the household during that time. Yet, I do remember that my younger brother was the one with my grandfather when he passed.

I truly believe that the extent of the experiences of so many of my loved ones dying, symbolizes some of the dark moments of my life. It is ironic that the passing of my paternal grandfather happened the same year that I gave birth to my daughter. The correlation that we hear, that someone dies and someone is born haunted me shortly after the birth of my daughter. There was a sacrifice of a life for the opportunity of a new life and a re-creation or continuation of love sharing for someone that I lost. I attribute the loss of loved ones, the loss of self-dignity during the domestic violence that I experienced, the loss of love for someone or even the ending of a relationship, as a form of "loss" carnally in terms; nevertheless, we can get through anything and all things in our lives, as long as we have faith and love for God. A colleague of mine told me it was appropriate to write a letter to someone close that has already passed on to be with the Lord or to write a letter to someone close that is still alive today. I could write so many letters to loved ones that I failed to express my feelings to prior to their death. Because I believed this principle, I decided to write a letter to my grandmother, who I have fond memories of, and to document some of the crucial times of my life, as I recall them. I was still pretty young; however, the memories that I have are still very vivid as I grow older. So here it goes. This letter is to my Maternal Grandmother, who was the first to die. We affectionately called her "Momma".

Dear Momma,
Seems like only yesterday, I can see your face as I remember you. I remember your firm, round face with the braids in your hair. I remember your firm smile, big eyes, brown complexion, tall, slim, meek and mild mannered.
I remember so vividly the nights and days that you would hold me in your arms and rock me to sleep. I was always in so much pain and uncomfortable because of the weight that the braces had on my legs. Sometimes, I would awaken in the middle of the night and just scream out. I remember times you appeared at my bedside and would comfort me. My sisters and brothers would always make fun of me, called me a cry baby and a cripple, but you would always call me

"peanut" and console me. I don't know why you called me "peanut", but it was soothing to my ear. I miss the touch of your hands and the comfort of your smile. Thank you for caring for me and loving me forever.
Love you,
Peanut

That lady, "Momma", who had such a profound impact in my life, taught me so much about life that I never really realized I had until I began to experience life as an adult. I do believe that if I had never had the experiences or exposure to a strong woman, as I saw in my grandmother, I would probably not have been able to deal with any of the obstacles that I endured in my life. I would have given up a long time ago, but I would always remember seeing the relationship that "Momma" and "Daddy" had, even though not always perfect, but respectful of one another. Daddy worked while Momma cooked, took care of the household, and disciplined the only way she knew how. Momma would discipline us; however, she would always assure us that even though she had to discipline us, she still loved us.

CHAPTER 8

"Count it all joy, my brothers (sisters), when you meet trials of various kinds, for you know that the testing of your faith produces steadfastness. And let steadfastness have its full effect, that you may be perfect and complete, lacking in nothing."James 1:2-4

Abuse to Life

Sometimes I look back and I wonder what my life would have been like if I never walked away from that abusive relationship. I asked myself the question, "If I had been abused all my life, how would I know that I Deserve Life? I immediately fell on my knees and I thank God for keeping me and helping me to get through the trials and tribulations of my life. I thank God for opening my eyes to the word and for the encouragement I received from my grand-mother when I was always ready to give up; the encouragement my grandmother gave me when I thought that I was not pretty enough or strong enough to walk on my own. My grandmother and my parents encouraged me to keep trying and as a result, I was able to walk without the braces. Even though I experienced abuse in my family and in my neighborhood so many different times and thought that it was normal for mothers and fathers to fight and make up, I realize now that the times in my life that I saw these activities going on, I never understood the impact it had on my mother, my grandmother, my sisters, my brothers, my cousins, my neighbors, or whomever. I believe "I Deserve Life" because after all the years that I experienced different situations, I committed my life, my heart and my soul to Jesus Christ. I began to read the word in order to obtain an understanding for myself of what God's expectations are of me and that I can only be responsible for me while doing what it is that God wants me to do; and how God wants me to treat others, take care of others and educate and feed my children and those who do not know Him for the free pardoning of their sins. I know now, that if I did not believe and trust God's word and walked away from the abusive relationship I was in, I would not be alive today to tell my story. "I Deserve Life", because I believe what the Bible says God has provided for my life. Jeremiah 29:11 states: *"For I know the plans for you says the Lord, plans to prosper you and not harm you. Plans to give you hope and a future".*

CHAPTER 9

"Do not be anxious about anything, but in everything by prayer and supplication with thanksgiving let your requests be made known to God. And the peace of God, which surpasses all understanding, will guard your hearts and your minds in Christ Jesus". Phil 4:6-7

Living a Good Life

I know that "I Deserve Life"; however, I think about what a good life looks like. I think about the fact that even though my life was sometimes abusive, poor or meaningless, does it mean that I did not have a good life or I did not "Deserve Life"? Because I Believe, it helps me to understand that the experiences I encountered were needed to get me to the point of my life where I am now. If I never had those specific life experiences, that I blocked out of my mind, I would not be able to appreciate the life that I have now since, I matured and connected my life, my heart and my soul to idolize God and to thank Him for His Grace and Mercies that He provides in my life everyday. I asked myself the question, "What does a good life look like?"

A good life to me is a life where I can be authentic, a life where I no longer fear anyone other than God. As I mature and commit my life to God, it helps me to understand and realize that as long as I trust God and continue to give God all the Honor and the Praise for each day of my life, I will have a "good life". As I have matured, I understand now that I am not perfect, that we are all sinners who fall short and I must continue to be a work in progress until I can get it right. I trust God for His word and for His wisdom. Every time I find myself going in the wrong direction, I pull back and sometimes I have to ask God to forgive me for the sins I have committed against Him and against my neighbor. Jesus died on the cross and sacrificed HIS life so that we might have life and have it more abundantly. Therefore, there is no man or woman that has the authority to take the life of another human being; no man or woman has the right to decide that you don't deserve life...whether it is a spouse, a perpetrator of domestic violence or anyone. God has given us the opportunity to be here and "*You Deserve Life...You Deserve to Live...You Deserve Life*".

CHAPTER 10

"I can do all things through him who strengthens me." Phil 4:13

How I Survived My Past

I wrote a letter to "Momma" because I believe that it was the impact "Momma" had on my life that helped me to survive the trials, tribulations, the abuse and the struggles I endured in my past. I thank God for my life experiences, my struggles and my abuse. I believe that God in His infinite wisdom took me through those times, through those struggles, and through those situations in order to teach me, and to make me strong. These encounters were also for me to gain the understanding and the wisdom that in going through and in coming out, I am to use these past sufferings to enable me to share my stories by giving first-hand experiences and situations "the light" needed to help others heal and understand that God kept me, and that God pulled me up out of the lowest and darkest days and nights of my life.

The times that I felt that I did not want to live any longer, those times, that I felt that I did not deserve to be on this earth or those times that I thought I would never be able to be successful or important to anyone or anything in my life...I remember those times that I did not know where the money was coming from, how

32

I was going to feed my children, pay my bills or how I was going to make it through the night. I prayed often; however, I did not know how to pray to God for what I thought I needed. I remembered the nights that I would walk into my grandmother's room or my mother's room and I would see them as they kneeled down by the side of their bed and prayed. It took me years to understand how important it was to pray to God each day, thanking Him for waking me up in the morning and praying to God at night to watch over me while I slept. But God...

I remember being embarrassed when I re-married about kneeling at night to pray. I am still a work in progress; the older I get the more relaxed and unafraid to let my spouse see me praying. I survived my past, because, my mother and grandmother never hesitated to pray or speak the word of God every time they had an opportunity. I understand that if I am going to be able to survive my past, I must continue to *forget those things that are behind and press on to the mark for the prize of the high calling in Christ Jesus* (Phil 3:13-14) and not be afraid or embarrassed to pray in front of anyone at anytime.

I continue to read the word, research the word, listen, and encourage the word, not only to myself, but to help others to receive the word. "Momma" comes to mind every time I begin to read the word and every time I being to speak the word to others. I believe that the only reason I was able to survive my past was because of the foundation that my grandmother and my parents gave me. As a little child, I remember going to Sunday school and Church every Sunday. I remember sometimes staying in church all day on Sundays. We would walk from one side of the city from our home to the other side of the city to get to church. I did not understand everything we were taught, but I knew that Sunday school or Church was not an option for us. I looked forward to attending church on Sundays. We saw it as a time to come together with our friends, but the music and singing that we experienced stuck with me for the rest of my life. As I got older, I never tarried away from Church because Church had become a part of my life. I followed the same foundation that my mother, my father and my grandparents instilled in me with my children, as well. Even though, once they got older and began to make decisions of their own, getting them to follow through was not as important to them as it was to me. However, I do believe that the foundation was instilled in them and hopefully they are instilling the same foundation in their children. Every opportunity that I have to teach and encourage my children, my grandchildren and my great grandchildren, I take advantage of the situation.

I know how important it is to teach our children and encourage others to seek the word of God. There is never a time, whenever the opportunity presents itself, that I don't speak about God and how God brought me through the worse times in my life. I proclaim His word every opportunity that I have, to witness to others that may be going through situations or challenges in their life, how I was able to get pass those obstacles in my life. I am not ashamed to share my story. I believe the word that my Testimony is a Test and sharing will help someone else to heal. I refuse to give up the rights that God has given me to endure. I refuse to give up my love and trust for God. I refuse to stop fighting to see what the end is going to bring. I know that God would never leave me nor will He forsake me. God gave me the courage to press on. I was born for a purpose and even though I hurt sometimes, I understand and know that God loves me and God has a purpose for my life.

I remember "Momma".

CHAPTER 11

"O LORD my God, you have performed many wonders for us. Your plans for us are too numerous to list. You have no equal. If I tried to recite all your wonderful deeds, I would never come to the end of them." Psalm 40:5

Strength to Pass the Test

"You Deserve Life', but do you have the "Strength to Pass the Test"? Everyday I wake up alive; I understand that it is my faith, dedication and respect for God that is being tested. I believe that we all have some Goliaths in our lives, people we think are there to help us, but instead they just keep bringing us down. I believed that "Momma" was my lifeline and her teachings and encouragement prepared me for many of the situations, trials and tribulations I have experienced. No matter what people call you or attempt to do to you, as long as you have God in your heart, you will be strong and have all the strength that you need to pass the test because *Greater is He that is in me than he that is in the world* (I John 4:4). Situations and challenges we come across in our life are only a test, a test to see whether or not you trust and believe the word. Life is a test to see whether or not you will have the fortitude to withstand anything that comes into your spirit, anything that comes into your life. As long as you know that your hands are too short to box with God, you have won the battle. Always remember that God has given you everything you need to pass the test. God has given you everything you need to fight the battle; all that is required of you is "*Faith, the size of a Mustard Seed*". You will overcome anything, anytime you take a test or encounter a challenge. God is Faithful. Sometimes, we have to get out of the way and let God take control of the situation. God will win every time. So, remember, you were born with the strength to fight, with the strength to endure, and with the strength to keep going. Prayer is the key to have a conversation with God when you are going through a battle, and when you are faced with a test. Do not let anyone take away your faith or your love for God. God is always there and we just have to trust Him to do everything He has promised He will do. I believe that God carried me through the lowest points of my life to show me and to prove to me that as long as I honored Him and gave Him the opportunity to take control of it, I was able to pass the test. Quitting is not an option for those who trust and believe in God. The "*Battle Is Not Yours, It's The Lords*". I had to be bold about what it is that God has put into my spirit. God chose me, even though I had to fight all of my life to get to that specific point in my life to trust and believe that God does have an awesome plan for my life. The Blessing is rightfully mine, despite what my abuser attempted to take away from me. I remember the day that he took everything I owned; all of my clothes and threw them in the dumpster around the corner from the house. He tried everything He could to tear me down and to break me. I remembered days that he would tell me that I was nothing and that I would never get anyone else in my life. Okay but today, I know without a doubt in my mind that whatever God has for me, is for me! I struggled in the past…I struggled through my abuse, and I struggled through the military, but God reminded me that for every tear that I shed, for every battle that I lost, every opportunity that I thought was for me, it all belongs to God and He has what is rightfully mine. I remember Momma and the things that she taught me. It gave me strength when I witnessed my mother's and my grandmother's vigor, because it's what kept me going. I continue to trust and believe, and although sometimes I fall short, but God continues to be faithful to me even when I am not.

CHAPTER 12

"Delight yourself in the LORD, and he will give
you the desires of your heart." Psalm 37:4

"You Deserve Life" – Claim It!!!!

If he never does anything else, he's already done enough. Because you don't know my story and all the things that I've been through, you cannot understand why I cry. It's not because I'm sad, but because my worship is for real. The tears you see are tears of joy because my spirit is rejoicing and giving God glory for bringing me through so many times, over and over again, so I say, "if God doesn't do another thing in my life, He's already done enough". God has been so good to me that I must worship Him, because the struggle is real and my worship is for real. Thank you, Jesus.

God Favored Me and I have a testimony, that God favored me despite of the curse of domestic violence that I encountered in my life. I can't help myself, when I think about all that God has done for me and how God has brought me through. I know that I was and am special in His eyes, because, I'm still here, I'm still alive, and I am still Blessed. God loves me. I went through a situation where my love was abused, where my body was abused, where my mind was abused and most of all my heart was abused. But because of my faith, God Favored Me and I know that God kept me.

We sometimes fall down in our life, but we get up. When we fall down, all we have to do is look up and trust God. I've come through many hard times in my life; I've fallen down and I've been to the point where I did not know how I was going to pay my bills. I've had days that I had to go on government assistance in order to feed my children, but I know that God was always there protecting me and God was always in the midst. There were times that I questioned God, and I asked, "where is God when love hurts?" If God claimed that He loved me and I was His child, why was I going through those dark days in my life? But God and God alone! I have not always had the strong faith that I have now; God had to take me through good times and bad times. I had mountains to climb and rivers to cross, but I persevered. I wandered around trying to find true love according to what I felt was true love. God allowed me to go from one relationship to another, but it wasn't until I gave my life to Christ and was ready to give up my sinful ways that I remarried and was able to find true love and satisfaction in a relationship with my spouse.

My daughter was eight and my son was a little over two years old. I shielded them away from the arguments and fights, which happened mostly at night when they were already asleep, when I was in the privacy of my bedroom or while they were at the sitters. Several of my girlfriends and I shared our stories just between us. Some spoke their truths, and of course others never did. My girlfriend would tell me that her husband did not hit her, but he would verbally abuse her. We would talk about it among ourselves, but never told anyone. We were afraid to leave because we knew that they were the men of the house; however, not necessarily the bread winners in the house. We all worked and sometimes I made just as much as he did or sometimes more. In fact, he would get complacent with his job, drink irresponsibly then sometimes he would get fired from the job. Well, we know that loss of the job, led to frustrations in the home; disagreements, fights, stealing and demanding my money with no consideration of the need to pay bills or just money sitting in the savings. Eventually, we would get to the point where there was not enough money to pay the bills, have food or pay the rent. We would experience evictions, utilities being turned off and food being an issue, as well. I remember times that I would have to hide money in the car or in my children's drawers so that he could not find it in my purse when he demanded. Sometimes, I would just be so tired of fighting or arguing that I would just give in to his demands. In the four and a half years of marriage, we must have moved at least 6-7 times because of evictions. I worked shift work while he would run and do whatever he wanted to do. I remember specific times that I would come home from work and either find the kids at home by themselves or not home at all. He would sometimes take them with him; Lord knows where and what he was doing. There were a couple of situations where he took them with him, broke the law, went to jail and had to call my brothers to come and pick the kids up from the Police Station until I was able to get off from work.

CHAPTER 13

"No, in all these things we are more than conquerors through him who loved us". Romans 8:37

The Beginning of A New Era

God sent me someone who loved me for who I am. Paul and I met and dated about nine years after all of the abuse happened in my life, but still I could not tell my story.

When I dated my husband, I was so very cautious because I did not want to end up in another abusive relationship. I broke off the relationship twice and it wasn't until I went to Basic Training and returned, to find him still waiting...then we married. He did not know my story, because I never told him. My children were grown, and other than what they remembered, they did not know my story. When I divorced my first husband, my children were very young. I stayed single for nine years after the divorce of my first marriage, so by the time I married my second husband, my daughter was 17 years old and my son was 11 years old. My now husband was a part of my children's lives during the courtship; however, the story never came out. I wanted to be sure that he was the man for me; therefore, I watched and observed the way he related to my children. For the most part, he was more of a father figure to them, especially to my son who was not accustomed to having a man around. He was two years old when his father and I divorced. My youngest daughter was born two years after I married her dad in 1992 and my oldest daughter had her first child at the age of 19, a month after my youngest daughter was born. I never told the story, because I was afraid that my husband might not accept it, I was ashamed and the fact that I thought it was my fault and should have done more to make the marriage work. Shortly after my daughter had her first child, she got pregnant with her second son and the drama began. Spats between her and her children's father sometimes mounted into arguments that led to my husband and I separating them to make peace. Still, the story never came out. My daughter and her friends, for the most part, were in relationships where there was some type of violence; verbal or physical abuse was prevalent. I always found myself going to their rescue and at least trying to talk and encourage them to let the relationship go, but to no avail, the more I pleaded and told them that the situation was not going to change, I still never gave any justification as to how I knew. My daughter had her third child, and then a fourth child, a daughter. Because of my shame, I never told my story. I wanted to be the saving grace for them, but I could not bring myself to telling them my story. After experiencing situations not only with my daughters, but with my daughter's friends, with my girlfriends and other family members, I guess, I along with them thought that this was normal behavior. Moreover, it happened when we were children and now that it was happening in our pre-teen, teenage and adult lives, it must be customary for relationships or marriages.

I learned from my previous marriage that the more you try to tell someone that is a victim of domestic violence, the more they will protect their abuser, make excuses for them and hide what is going on. Until the person that is experiencing abuse makes up in their minds that they don't want to remain in that situation, there is nothing you can tell them. If you nag at them, they will either isolate themselves or their mate will isolate them from you so that you can't encourage them to leave or get out of the situation.

Isolation is one of the first forms of domestic violence. They isolate you from your friends and your family so you are not able to tell anyone what is occurring. I recall a girlfriend of mine was being abused by her boyfriend, prior to her marrying him. I remember how close we were and all of what we talked about. I remember the conversations that we had about how she was being abused by her boyfriend and that we knew from experiences that he would never changed. Even though we spoke about each other's experiences, she still married him, despite the warnings we spoke about. We continued to hang out after I had separated and divorced my ex-husband to comfort and support each other, once I married my second husband. They were dating and we would talk about some of what she was going through. Other friends and I would share the things that we had all gone through in previous relationships. There were three of us and for sake of privacy, I will name them Shea and Angie. I remember Shea, Angie and I would get together, talk and laugh about any and everything. We would have conversations about our relationships and generally about men. I remember so clearly a conversation we had one day where we all vowed to investigate if anyone ever proclaimed that one of us committed suicide, because that would not be true.

Fast forward - about a year later, my friend Shea announced that she was marrying her then abusive boyfriend. We grew concerned, but of course, we could not change her mind. Fast forward - a year after the marriage, contact grew distant and communication even further away. We would call and check on her, sometimes to no avail. If he was around when she answered the telephone, she never said much because he would listen to what she was saying to us. If he answered the telephone, and realized it was one of us, he refused to let either of us speak to her. They had a son and a couple of years later I heard that she had twin girls. We talked and she sent me pictures, however, he would not let her come around or allow us to come around her. After the twins were born, we talked a little more, even though the relationship of seeing and visiting each other had grown to almost never seeing one another at all. Shea was so happy and proud of her son and her twin girls. I never had an opportunity to see the twins until two years later when Shea's mother died. We went to the funeral and as I sat in the church along side the family, I saw Shea motion up to the casket like she was in a deep trance. I noticed that she stood at the casket for a few minutes and just stood there over her mom. I wanted to console her, but her then husband went up to the casket and walked her back to her seat. I remember being saddened by what I had just witnessed. I could not wait until after the funeral with hopes of being able to comfort her and talk to her. We all gathered at her mom's house waiting for her to arrive; however she never did. He took her home and did not allow her to return to the house where friends and family were waiting to see and talk to her. I remember being so upset that I called to check on her and of course, he would not let me talk to her. Fast forward - I received a call from her inviting me to stop by the house to attend the fourth birthday party of her son. I remember it was in July and for some reason I was not able to attend, but we spoke that after-noon while the party was finishing up and she told me that she was cleaning up, then planned to lay out the kids clothes in preparation for church that next day. She was so happy about taking the kids to church on Sunday. Since the passing of her mother, less than five months or so prior, she would be able to celebrate being a mother even though her mother had passed on. Since her mother passed earlier in the year, Shea was still grieving on Mother's Day and this was the first Sunday that she was ready to take a step and take the twins and her son to church. We also talked about celebrating her birthday later in the week before we hung up the phone. Very early the next morning, I received a phone call from Shea's sister telling me that Shea's husband, I will call him Lenny, called and asked her if Shea had come by the house. We both thought the question and the conversation was sort of strange, but we began calling other family members and wondering where she might had gone. Fast forward - later that morning, her sister called me back and stated that Lennie told her that he remembered that Shea had gotten up around 4:30 a.m. to get a bottle for the twins; however, he fell back to sleep and did not realize once he woke up around 6:00 a.m. that Shea was not in the house. Lennie claimed that Shea had been so distressed about the passing of her mother and would visit her mom's grave a lot. He assumed she had gone to the gravesite to visit her mom, because she was still struggling with grieving the loss of her mother. Lennie claimed that he got dressed, drove to the gravesite to see if she was there, but did not find her there. He then claimed that as he was coming back across the bridge, he spotted Shea's car under the bridge (mind you, driving across this particular bridge, you can't really see what or if cars are down there). Anyhow, Lennie claimed he turned around and went down under the bridge where he saw her car, but she was not in it. Lennie claimed he called the police. Not to go into details about it, but it was a few days later, even though I did not believe that she just walked into that river and killed herself, Shea's body was found clear across the river on the opposite side of Charleston near a Marina. The coroner ruled the death accidental; however, Angie, her family nor I believed that she killed herself. I reminisced on the conversation we had about investigating if someone ever told one of us the other committed suicide to please investigate. The scene at her funeral was very solemn and Lennie would not or could not look any of us in the eyes. After the funeral, he isolated the kids from the family for several years after and of course that was the last time either Angie or I saw them. I recently ran across a picture of the kids and inquired with one of their aunts about how they are and she has promised to get me in touch with them after the COVID-19 Pandemic dies. I truly believe that this tragedy is what prompted me to share my story almost 35 years later and to be a witness to others going through DOMESTIC VIOLENCE. Even though the coroner ruled the death accidental, I believed and still believe in my heart that if he didn't put her in that river, he drove her to it. He was so dominating, verbally abusive to her and he always told her that she was not good enough or she was not pretty enough. Shea was very meticulous and organized and as I listened to the details of how he told the story, I could not believe any of what he said because I knew it was the total opposite of who she was. I prayed to God for forgiveness in my heart for him. But God...

After 2017, when I began to tell my story, I am more convinced that it had to be told in sequence to help others to heal. We are no way close to preventing these situations from happening, but God has put it in my spirit to confess, share my testimony, and lead others to seek refuge in His word by persistently taking a bold stand to end the senseless killing and manipulation of one human being to another. Less than 4 years ago, I experienced the tragic killing of my girlfriend's 15 year old granddaughter who was shot and killed by her 17 year old boyfriend. Two weeks later, another friend's 23 year old daughter, whom was also a friend with my then 23 year old daughter, was killed by her live-in boyfriend.

I promised God that I will not stop sharing my story, I will not be ashamed to be a witness for God to show others that if they just trust God, be obedient to God, honor God and praise God that He will bring you out of whatever situation you may find yourself in. Just pray to God and ask him to protect you, and pray to God and ask him to bring you through what you're going through. God is able to do all things. If you surrender your life to Christ and ask God to be there for you, He will. We must be reminded that we have been chosen to set our own interests aside, let go of our own ambitions, and face the enemy full-on. God has given each of us a job, a position, resources, education and so much more. God has opened doors and opportunities to optimize His Kingdom's purposes. He's placed us wherever we are because we are in the midst of a battle, a war. You and I are in the midst of a seismic conflict involving good versus evil. To miss a kingdom assignment because we've become too caught up in our personal kingdom is one of the greatest trage-dies we could ever face.

I don't know why God seemingly has to keep taking us through things over and over again before we get the message. I just know that God takes us through and He allows us to suffer until we give in and surrender our will to God's will. When we let go, He will take care of the situation and it is then that His Glory can be revealed through us. God sees the best in us. I forgave my ex-husband a long time ago before he left this earth. I never held any malice in my heart for him and I never spoke evil about him to my children. I thank God for the struggle, as his glory was revealed to make me, The Woman Behind The Mask, which I am today. When God favors you, God is positioning you in a place and time (such as this) to be ready when God needs you and when God is ready to use you to be a servant or blessing to others. When God Favors us, He has already prepared us for the things that the enemy has put in front of us. What the enemy set for evil, God has already blessed us for good. Favor is always a precursor to a fight. When God blesses you, he puts you there to be ready for the fight that is about to come. I Believe That, For Such A Time As This - God has Favored Me and all those around me to establish this platform to share God's words, to motivate and lift up the spirits of Women all over this world.

The Women of God, spirit-filled, rich in spirit... But God. The woman who is successful; The Woman who is loved; The Woman who is educated; The Woman who has a beautiful family; The Woman who is respected by many; The Woman who never gave up on God; The Woman Behind The Mask that is beginning the next chapter of her life. *"Perhaps this is the moment for which you have been created."* - *Esther 4:14 NKJV*; **Yes,** I do believe that "**You Deserve Life**!"

Psalm 51:17 17 "My sacrifice, O God, is a broken spirit; a broken and contrite heart you, God, will not despise.

Hebrews 13:15-17 15 Through Jesus, therefore, let us continually offer to God a sacrifice of praise- the fruit of lips that openly profess his name. 16 And do not forget to do good and to share with others, for with such sacrifices God is pleased. 17 Have confidence in your leaders and submit to their authority, because they keep watch over you as those who must give an account. Do this so that their work will be a joy, not a burden, for that would be of no benefit to you.

John 3:16 16 For God so loved the world that he gave his one and only Son, that whoever believes in him shall not perish but have eternal life.

Romans 12:1-2 1 Therefore, I urge you, brothers and sisters, in view of God's mercy, to offer your bodies as a living sacrifice, holy and pleasing to God-this is your true and proper worship. 2 Do not conform to the pattern of this world, but be transformed by the renewing of your mind. Then you will be able to test and approve what God's will is-his good, pleasing and perfect will". KJV

ABOUT THE AUTHOR

Jeremiah 29:11
"For I know the plans I have for you," declares
the LORD, "plans to prosper you and not to harm
you, plans to give you hope and a future".

Karen Wright-Chisolm grew up in Charleston, South Carolina, the 7th child of eleven children, born to the late Benjamin Wright and the Late Adell Meyers Wright both of Charleston, S.C. Karen attended the public schools of Charleston and graduated from Burke High School in 1973. Karen is a Retired Veteran of 27 years, 8 months and 14 days from the United States Air Force, retiring as a Chief Master Sergeant, the highest enlisted rank only obtained by 1 % of the force. Karen is also retired from Civil Service with over 21 years of service as a civil service employee. Karen is noted as being the first black and first female to serve as Superintendent of the 315th Mission Support Squadron on the Charleston Air Force Base. Karen's principal duties included leading and mentoring airmen on the importance of professional military education for a successful military career. Karen's last 4 years on Active Duty was served at the Pentagon.

While at the Pentagon, her principal duties included Superintendent, Headquarters; United States Air Force Air Staff, assigned to the Pentagon, Washington, District of Columbia. Her duties included translating Department of Defense (DOD), HQ, USAF, and USAFR policies and decisions into workable plans of action. Chief Chisolm advised the Chief, Systems and Analysis, Director of Personnel, and Chief of Air Force Reserve on matters pertinent to military systems programs and data systems supporting the Office of Air Force Reserve. Karen worked directly with division chiefs and their staffs, OSDS, Air Staff, HQ AFPC, HQ AFRC, HQ ARPC and other Reserve Components to ensure personnel program management actions were in compliance with law, DOD, USAF, and USAFR guidance. Chief Chisolm interacted daily with OSD, Air Staff, Joint Staff, NGB, and Headquarters Staff of sister services, HQ AFRC, AFPC, and ARPC.

Mrs. Wright-Chisolm's professional education includes: Doctoral of Management Candidate, Ambassador Bible College and Seminary, Doctoral Management Candidate, Organizational Leadership – University of Phoenix, Dual Masters of Art Degree in Human Resources Management/Human Resources Development, Webster University; B.S. Degree in Human Resources Management, Southern Wesleyan University and Associate of Arts Degree in Human Resource Management/Personnel Administration, Community College of the Air Force (CCAF). Her principle awards and decorations include: Meritorious Service Medal with one device, Air Force Commendation Medal, Air Force Achievement Medal with two oak leaf clusters, Air Force Outstanding Unit Award with six devices, Air Reserve Forces Meritorious Service Award with five devices, National Defense Service Medal with one device, Global War on Terrorism Service Medal, Military Outstanding Volunteer Service Medal with one device, Air Force Longevity Service Award with four devices, Armed Forces Reserve Medal with 1 "M" device and bronze hourglass, USAF NCO PME Graduate Ribbon with 1 device and Air Force Training Ribbon and Civil Service Award.

Karen is a life member and Trustee of Greater St. Luke AME Church, Charleston, S.C. Karen is a Diamond Life Member of Delta Sigma Theta, Inc.; Life Member of TuskegeeAirmen; Board Member - Imperial Court Daughters Auxiliary; A.E.A.O.N.M.S., Inc., & Past Commandress of Arabian Court #128; Executive Board of the Charleston Branch N.A.A.C.P.; Regional Coordinator for the State Branch of NAACP; Jack & Jill; Past Matron of Eastern LightChapter No. 360 OES; Past Grand Associate Deputy for State Grand Chapter O.E.S., Past State Grand Loyal Lady Ruler and Past Loyal Lady Ruler, Order of Golden Circle, Reserve Enlisted

Associated, Inc.; AF Sergeants Association; Executive Board Member of C.O. Federal Credit Union, Executive Board and Chairperson of the Advisory Board of Jenkins Institute for Children; founder of Boots-2-Heels, Inc. South Carolina Chapter and a Board Member – Boots-2-Heels, Inc.; Member of the City of Charleston Women and Minority Business EnterpriseAdvisory Board; and Member of Veterans Upward Bound Advisory Board. Currently, Karen is an advocate and public speaker of Domestic Violence and is an Author who has contributed to two books along with other female authors, which have been noted as #1 Best Selling Authors, Sisters Silent No More – **"You Deserve Life"**; Authors of the 2nd book in which, Karen is a part of - Camouflaged Sisters – Leadership through the Eyes of Senior Military Women Leaders – **"Mentoring Is Critical to Success"** and was recently recognized as #1 Best Selling Authors, Amazon Bestselling Authors, Amazon Hot New Release, #1 in United States, Military Veterans History, #1 in

United States Veterans History, #3 in Military & Spies Biographies & #5 in Business Leadership.

Karen is married to Paul Chisolm, Jr. of Charleston, South Carolina and they are proud parents of four children, Tamara Brown, Eric Brown, Jr., Paul Chisolm, III and Jazmine Wright-Chisolm; proud grandparents of Shaquille, Nakearah, Traequan, Destiny, Caleb (deceased) Sanaa, William, and Rhyanne Heavenly Grace; great-grandparents of Sebastian, Ariah, and Amira.

Karen loves God and family. Karen's favorite scripture is Proverbs 3: 5-6, NIV; "Trust in the Lord" with all Thine heart, and lean not on your own understanding; in all your ways submit to him, and he will make your paths straight."

Her motto is: "Never Underestimate the Power of Someone Else's Struggles Unless You Have Walked in their Shoes".

Made in the USA
Columbia, SC
19 March 2022

57879366R00037